32 BADA$$ THINGS ABOUT BEING SOBER

SARAH ORDO

32 BADA$$ THINGS ABOUT BEING SOBER

COVER ART © SHAWNA POLIZIANI
SHAWNAPOLIZIANI.COM

ISBN: 9781091883000

I'm so f***ing excited for you.

Not only because you found this book...but also because you are clearly either interested in sobriety or already have chosen to be sober. Which means you have at some point struggled with alcohol (or still do).

I get it. I've been there.

I've woken up lying in a hospital bed hooked up to so many IVs, wires, and machines that I lost count. Why? Because there was a time in my life where I abused drugs and alcohol to the point that I almost didn't make it out alive.

Alcoholism, addiction, and substance abuse of any kind can absolutely destroy you. They can ruin your life, tear apart your relationships, and leave you feelings worthless, hopeless, and helpless.

When you find yourself in that place, you have two options: you fight like hell to get sober, or you accept your life the way it is.

FIGHT. I hope you fight like hell.

In this book, I'm highlighting thirty-two BADA$$ things about being sober. Because sobriety doesn't suck...and sometimes it's nice to be reminded of all the amazing, positive things it can do for you and for your life.

When it gets hard, read this book again. Or pass it on to someone else that might need the motivation and a reminder of why they are fighting the fight still.

Remember all the times you woke up feeling like you just got hit by a f*ing bus?**

The pounding head, the sweaty skin, and feeling physically ill to the point you can't even lift your head up off of the pillow, the floor, the stranger's couch cushion, or wherever else you passed out at the night before. Abusing alcohol makes you feel like absolute s***.

Was it worth it? HELL NO.

When I think about how often I wasted an entire day hungover and sick from the previous night's binge, I can't believe how much of my life I wasted being sick. I would waste at least half of the day chugging water, popping Tums and pain relievers like they were candy, and curling myself up into the fetal position in hopes that the miserable feeling would just pass quickly.

Now you get to wake up feeling rested, refreshed, and ALIVE.

Think about how amazing it is to wake up in the morning feeling AMAZING. Waking up to see the sunrise with a cup of freshly brewed coffee. Going out for a run. Meeting a friend for brunch. You get to wake up each morning present, feeling f***ing amazing, and ready to face the day head on.

You get to wake up with another day of sobriety under your belt.

2. having a FATTER wallet

How many times did you cringe at your bar tab when closing time rolled around?

Y'all know that feeling. You carelessly told the bartender, "Yes, I'd love to open a tab!" and then regretted it immediately once it was time to cash out. It seemed easy to just open that tab and yell to your friends that the next round was on you after you were a few shots deep. Then again, you probably didn't even know how much you paid up until the next day when you looked at your banking account.

Maybe not your smart investment.

It's always been pretty convenient for us ladies to count on the men at the bar to pay for our drinks, but I somehow ALWAYS walked out spending a sh*t ton of money, regardless. I realized just how much money I was spending on drinking only after I stopped. It was like "DAMN! What can I do with all this extra money now!?"

Now you can spend that money on things that make you feel truly happy.

Want to go on an amazing vacation? BOOK IT! Want to treat yourself to concert tickets? BUY 'EM! With all the money you're saving on the alcohol you're not drinking, you can invest it in living your best life now.

Invest that money in things that make you feel ALIVE again.

How many times did you cringe at your bar tab when closing time rolled around?

Y'all know that feeling. You carelessly told the bartender, "Yes, I'd love to open a tab!" and then regretted it immediately once it was time to cash out. It seemed easy to just open that tab and yell to your friends that the next round was on you after you were a few shots deep. Then again, you probably didn't even know how much you paid up until the next day when you looked at your banking account.

Maybe not your smart investment.

It's always been pretty convenient for us ladies to count on the men at the bar to pay for our drinks, but I somehow ALWAYS walked out spending a sh*t ton of money, regardless. I realized just how much money I was spending on drinking only after I stopped. It was like "DAMN! What can I do with all this extra money now!?"

Now you can spend that money on things that make you feel truly happy.

Want to go on an amazing vacation? BOOK IT! Want to treat yourself to concert tickets? BUY 'EM! With all the money you're saving on the alcohol you're not drinking, you can invest it in living your best life now.

Invest that money in things that make you feel ALIVE again.

3. knowing what YOU DID last night

Nobody actually enjoys waking up and having no clue what the f*** happened.

Sure, you've probably laughed it off before. You've tried to make it humorous that you have no idea what you did the morning after a wild night out. You've struggled to piece back together the events of the night before...because you couldn't actually remember ANY of them. It was all just a blank night. No memories. No knowledge. No anything.

Have you ever thought about how bad things could have been?

I was the queen of laughing off my blacked-out nights and bragging about my crazy evenings out. At some point, I began to realize just how dangerous this was. I started to realize that having no idea what I did the night before meant that horrible things could happen to me and I would be helpless.

How wonderful does it feel waking up without amnesia from the night before?

Waking up knowing exactly where you were, what you did, and who you were with might not seem like a huge deal initially, but when you realize all the times you didn't...it will be extremely eye-opening. You'll know everything that happened. No gaps. No blanks. No wondering or questioning.

You were present. You were safe. You knew exactly what you were doing.

4. feeling HEALTHY

Alcohol can wreak absolute havoc on the body.

Alcohol is a toxic, aggressive substance that effects you on the outside and on the inside. If you've abused alcohol for any amount of time, you've probably experienced some of the effects firsthand. Alcohol can absoluely destroy your body. From cirrhosis of the liver to jaundice skin and eyes to inflammation in the bloodstream...alcohol attacks our bodies when it is abused for any amount of time.

Physical deterioaration is not uncommon in alcoholics.

During my mid-twenties, I began to experience my first physical symptoms of my alcohol consumption. I had chronic inflammation throughout my body. Numerous x-rays, blood work panels, and tests for autoimmune diseases all came back negative. Something else was attacking my body and turning my body against itself...and it was the amount of alcohol I was consuming.

How amazing does it feel to finally FEEL healthy?

After abusing our bodies with alcohol for years, it is time to finally heal and take care of them. It is time to treat them with respect and care. Exercise. Eat nourishing foods. Grow stronger. Give yourself rest. It's time to FEEL healthy again.

It's time to heal our bodies.

5. REAL friendships

Alcohol has a way of convincing you that EVERYONE is your best friend.

Y'all know what I'm talking about. Suddenly you love everyone, and everyone is your bestie. Don't even get me started on drunk girls in the bathroom. It's like we've known each other since we were babies...watching each other pee, holding each other's hair back, taking selfies in the dirty bathroom mirror. Y'all know eaxctly what I'm talkng about.

What happens when the alcohol gets removed from the equation?

I lost some of who I thought were my "best friends" when I got sober. It was a rude awakening of who was going to stick around still when the good times with alcohol weren't there anymore. It hurt. It was super disappointing. But you know what I learned? REAL friends will be by your side whether alcohol and the party is still happening or not.

The friendships you keep in sobriety are worth their weight in gold.

When you are sober, you start to see who your real, deep-rooted friendships are. You learn who was just around for the fun and who was around because they genuinely care about you. Cherish the ones that stuck around through the good, the messy, the ugly, and the transformation. They are the keepers that love you for YOU.

Real friends will love you through all the stages of your life.

6. more MENTAL clarity

Sobriety sometimes feels like someone turned the lights back on.

Alcohol has a way of clouding our mind, our judgement, and especially our mental clarity more than we may even be aware of sometimes. You just don't think clearly when your brain and consciousness are muddled down by alcohol. It's like you're living life through a hazy cloud that makes it difficult to see and think about things rationally.

When you stop drinking, your brain starts working differently.

Once I stopped drinking, it was like I finally gained the mental clarity I thought I had all along. I didn't even realized how dumbed down and foggy my thinking was. It was like someone turned the lights back on, opened my eyes, and made things clear again. I could finally think clearly and more rationally. Hallelujah!

You will be shocked at how much your mental clarity improves.

Your brain will regain the ability to be laser-focused and sharp when you are no longer abusing alcohol. Think of all of the things this could enable you to do. Want to start that business? Want to chase after that crazy dream? Want to share your story? Write a book? Change your whole life? NOW YOU CAN.

Everything and anything is possible when you're thinking clearly again.

7. sober SEX

What's the point of having drunk sex when you won't remember it anyways?

You've seen it in the movies, you've heard your friends share stories about it, you've probably done it yourself...drunk sex. It's crazy and wild and fun, right? It could be. But it also could be careless, dangerous, and something you won't even remember, too. Drunk sex can be no big deal, but it also can be a VERY big deal.

Have you ever had drunk sex that you regretted?

There were so many times I woke up crying and regretting what I had done and who Id done it with. There were times I didn't even remember one second of it. There were times I was careless that could have ended in disease or unintended pregnancies. There were even times that things happened to me that I did not consent to. That is the dangerous but VERY real side of drunk sex.

Imagine having sex with emotion and intention attached to it again.

This is not saying to save yourself for marriage. This is not saying you can't have casual, fun, consensual sex. This is not saying you have to become a nun and swear off of sex altogether. But, this is saying that sober sex can be amazing, beautiful, and something you'll want to actually remember.

Sober sex is just f*ing awesome. PERIOD.**

8. feeling in CONTROL

When alcohol takes control, we lose control.

When you struggle with addiction or abuse any addictive substance or behavior, you've essentially lost the ability to have control over it. Sure, there may be some people out there that can control their use or their behaviors. For those that struggle with addiction...they might never be able to exercise such control.

What have you lost by allowing alcohol to take over control?

There are many things in my life that happened as a result of my losing control. When alcohol took over, I stopped caring about things I once cared about, I stopped thinking about the consequences of my choices, and I ultimately lost control of my life on a regular basis. I was no longer in the driver's seat of my own life, alcohol had completely taken over.

What will you do with the control you take back?

The possibilities of what you can do, be, and achieve when you get back in control of your life are limitless. YOU get to choose what you will do. YOU get to choose how you will feel. YOU get to have control over your entire life again. What will you do with that control and power now that you have found it again?

You are back in control and back in the driver's seat of your life.

9. finding your PERSONALITY again

You aren't yourself anymore when you're drunk.

This isn't a shocker to anyone that has ever had a drink. Alcohol has the ability to turn you into someone that you are not. It creates a new personality for you and turns you into someone that you don't even recognize. This is why so many people are embarrassed or ashamed of the things they do while under the influence...alcohol makes them act in ways that they would not choose to while they are sober.

You become someone that you don't like or want to be.

Many mornings I cringed at the things I did while I was drunk. I would think about things I said and wonder where the hell they came from. I would feel sick from the embarrassment I felt about how I behaved. I became someone that I did not like at all. I took on the personality of someone that I did not want to be.

It's time to regain control over who you are.

Each and every one of us has a unique and individual personality that makes us who we are. When we are drunk, we lose that person. Alcohol causes us to lose that person. We no longer have to lose ourselves. We get to show the word our beautiful personality and who we really are. Finding yourself again and rediscovering who you are is an absolute gift.

Welcome back.

10.REAL courage, NOT liquid courage

Alcohol gives us liquid courage, not real courage.

We've all been in a situation where we may have leaned on alcohol a little bit too much to give us a boost of confidence or courage. We've all had that drink before a date to "loosen up" or calm our nerves a bit. But the courage that alcohol gives us is temporary, an act, and short-lived. It doesn't last.

When have you used drinking to get that liquid courage boost?

I have always been a bit of an extrovert, but alcohol gave the me the feeling that I was a bad*** b**** when I was out at the bar. Alcohol made me feel more confident, boosted my ability to approach men, and I relied on it heavily to feel good about myself. The problem with my doing that was that it never lasted. The courage wasn't real, it was only surface-level liquid courage.

Real courage will last.

You can find the courage within yourself now. You can know that the confidence you feel is REAL, and that it won't fade away as the alcohol wears off. You now have the chance to feel stronger, hold your head a little bit higher, and face your life with REAL courage. The kind of courage that doesn't fade away once you sober up.

What will you do will the REAL courage you gain?

11. having SOBER fun

You can still have fun sober.

So many people are fearful of missing out on fun in life when they get sober. It's "FOMO" times a million. The truth is, there is NOTHING about being sober that limits your fun in life. There is nothing you will enjoy any less in life just because you don't have a drink in your hand. You can still have just as much (if not MORE) fun while sober as you did when you were drinking.

Sobriety doesn't need to be a buzzkill.

When I got sober, I actually remember asking myself, "So, what do I do now?" when the weekends would roll around. How pathetic, right? There are SO many things you can do while sober. There are so many places you can go, things you can see, and people you can meet. I realized that there was nothing about being sober that limited how much fun I was able to have.

Fun might look very different to you now.

Odds are that the things you consider to be fun when you were drunk might not be fun anymore when you're sober. You'll quickly realize that the alcohol wasn't the thing that was making you have fun. It's the people, places, and experiences in our lives that create the fun. It's truly living your life to the fullest that creates the most enjoyment.

Now go out there and have some REAL fun!

12. making your OWN decisions

Why the f*** did I decide to do that!?

When alcohol takes over, you loose all ability to make choices for yourself. It's very difficult to make rational, level-headed decisions when you are wasted. Everything seems like a great idea no matter how dangerous, risky, or bad it might be. We are not the best decision makers when we are under the influence. But I'm sure you already knew that from experience, right?

You lose the power to think rationally when you're drunk.

If I had a dollar for every morning I woke up regretting the decisions I made the night before, I would have been living in a mansion by the time I was twenty-five years old. The decisions I made while drunk were ones that I would NEVER make sober. This only led me to feel regret, embarrassment, and like things were always out of control in my life.

Sobriety puts you back in control.

Once you are sober, you take back the decision-making power that you once gave away. It's now up to you again. YOU get to decide what you want to do. YOU get to decide where you want to go. YOU get to decide what kind of life you want to live. You've taken that power away from alcohol and given it back to yourself.

Decide to live your life again.

13. more self-RESPECT

Abusing alcohol is not showing yourself respect.

When we are consuming large amounts of alcohol, we are not respecting our bodies. But this idea doesn't only come into play regarding our physical bodies. What is an even bigger issue is the respect we lack in showing ourselves. This can be reflected in our actions and the choices we make while our inhibitions are lowered or non-existant.

We treat ourselves in ways that are disrespectful.

The amount of respect I lacked toward myself while drunk was extremely obvious when it came to my behavior towards the opposite sex. I would put my body on display to attract men and sleep with people I didn't care about just for the attention. I had no respect for myself, my body, or my well-being. It made me feel absolutely terrible.

It's time to show ourselves more respect.

It's time we treat ourselves with the utmost respect possible...physically, emotionally, and mentally. It's time to create a life in sobriety where we treat ourselves as we deserve to be treated. And we deserve to be treated with respect, love, and compassion. We deserve the self-respect we deprived ourselves of for all that time we spent drinking.

Respect yourself for the amazing human being that you are.

14. actually FEELING things again

Many people use alcohol to not feel things.

Alcohol does a great job of blocking out the s*** that we don't want to feel or deal with. It often seems much easier to say "I need a drink..." than to actually process and work through things that feel undesirable, difficult, or traumatic. Alcohol is seen as a quick fix answer, but it doesn't actually fix anything. It simply drowns and numbs our feelings away until later when they resurface again.

Numbing yourself from your feelings is not healthy.

I used alcohol to attempt to numb my anxiety, depression, and the traumatic experiences of my past for years. I also used alcohol to not deal with things happening in my life. Eventually I just started to feel numb from everything. I felt cold, numb, and blank until I got sober. In sobriety, I felt everything again. I felt alive again.

Allow all of the feelings to come back to you.

When you stop numbing out all of your feelings with alcohol, you might become overwhelmed when they all come rushing back in. There's a whole lot of things to feel. Appreciate the feelings, good and bad, because at least you are FEELING them again. At least you are healthy, alive, and living.

Feel every little thing.

15. decreased ANXIETY

A lot of us feel like we can ease anxiety with alcohol.

If you struggle with anxiety (or depression), then you know that it's NOT easy. We try to find ways to get through it and make it not feel as bad. Maybe a drink would help take the edge off? Maybe a buzz will mellow things out a bit? Not only does alcohol NOT treat or reduce anxiety, it's been proven that it can actually make it worse.

Anxiety can actually decrease the less that you drink.

I didn't realize just how much anxiety impacted my life until I got sober. Why? Because I never allowed myself to feel and deal with it. Once I got sober, I learned how to actually understand it, work through it, and reduce it. My anxiety has decreased more and more the longer that I've been sober. Coincidence? I don't think so.

Get your mental and emotional health back to a better place.

Once you get comfortable with yourself and do the self work, your anxiety will be much less intense. Now that you're sober, you're also able to take care of yourself, your emotional health, and your mental health much better. You'll feel the difference more and more with each day that passes.

It's time to breathe easy again.

16. a good night's SLEEP

Alcohol f∗∗∗s up your sleep big time.

Not only does waking up with a hangover make you feel like s∗∗∗, but sleeping after getting drunk is NOT good sleep. Alcohol makes you pass out, disrupts your body's natural sleep cycle, and often wakes you up super early after its "downer" effect wears off. The result? Waking up tired, groggy, and feeling drained all day long.

As if the "morning after" feeling wasn't bad enough already.

A girl loves her beauty sleep. Let's be honest, everyone just loves sleep. I never realized how bad my sleep was while I was drinking until I got sober. Once I felt what a restful, refreshing night of good sleep felt like, I realize how much alcohol had been f∗∗∗ing up mine for years. Not cool.

Going to bed early? Yes, please.

Get ready for the best sleep of your life, people! When you're sober, you don't have to deal with alcohol messing with your body's natural sleep schedule and cycle. You can have an amazing night of sleep.You're about to get the BEST sleep of your life. Grab your pillow, put on your pajamas, and enjoy!

It's time to start a love affair... with your bed.

17. looking HEALTHY

Alcohol doesn't only effect you on in inside.

Sometimes you can actually see it on someone's face when they are a heavy drinker. Sunken eyes, dark circles, jaundice skin, early wrinkles, dehydration...I don't know about you, but that's not a desirable look for most people. Alcohol not only damages your body on the inside, but you will start to see its effects on the outside, too.

The effects of alcohol go much farther than we often realize.

The first thing I saw changing when I got sober was my face. People actually commented on how I looked different. My skin looked smoother, glowy, and more youthful. My eyes looked brighter and more alive. My body shed the "puffy weight" that I used to gain from empty calories. Everything about my physical appearance just looked healthier in general, and it was very obvious to see.

Be good to yourself on the inside and you'll see it on the outside.

You will start to see yourself change on the outside quite quickly after getting sober. Get ready to look healthy, youthful, and absolutely beaming from the inside out. Removing alcohol from the inside will absolutely show on the outside. And who doesn't want to look f***ing amazing!?

Get ready to not only feel, but SEE the glow up!

18. challenging the SOCIETAL NORM

Society has turned drinking into the norm.

Everywhere you look today, there seems to be alcohol. The problem is not that it is available, the problem is that society has made it into something that seems normal to do on a daily basis. Things like happy hours after work, bottomless mimosa brunches, and wine being called "mommy juice" just enforce this idea that daily drinking is the norm today.

It's time to challenge the norm.

I never realized how much society glorifies drinking until I got sober. Once I stopped drinking, I realized that alcohol is EVERYWHERE. From social media to television to restaurants, drinking is glorified and often encouraged. Even the ads that pop up online for wine glasses that hold an entire bottle of moscato and flasks disguised as jewelry make it clear how normalized society has made alcohol consumption.

Let's create a NEW societal norm.

Now that you are sober, you get to challenge the f*** out of this societal norm. You get to prove that you can still have brunch without the booze. You can still wind down after a long day without half a bottle of wine. Let's change the norm. Let's change the way people see drinking. Let's start a f***ing movement.

Getting drunk doesn't need to be the norm.

19. finding your BEST LOVE

Alcohol clouds your judgment in all areas.

We've all been blinded by not only love, but also by alcohol while looking for love. We already know how much you're judgement is f***ed up when you're drunk. This can mean picking the wrong types of men and women. That only leads to heartbreak, unhealthy relationships, and regretful flings. You aren't seeing if your long term goals and morals are aligned with someone else's when you're looking for love drunk.

It's time to look for the RIGHT one.

The men I dated before I was sober were not exactly the cream of the crop. Now, all of them weren't bad apples, just to clarify. But I had a bad habit of letting my drunk self pick 'em. Not a good idea. I wasn't looking for the important qualities I needed from a man, I was looking at who was the hottest guy at the bar. I didn't meet the love of my life until I was sober, and I think that speaks pretty loudly.

Get ready for the BEST love.

Being able to meet someone amazing and connect with them with a clear head is golden. You can see past all of the surface level bulls*** and see the deeper stuff...the good stuff. You will realize what you want and what you don't want. You will decide what you will allow into your life and what you won't. You'll be able to find your best love.

It's time for the kind of love you deserved all along.

20. the SOBER community

There are people out there just like you.

The sober community is bigger than you probably ever realized. There are so many people in the wold working on getting healthy and becoming the best versions of themselves without alcohol. This community is one of the most welcoming, accepting, and supportive groups of humans you will ever meet in your life.

You may have lost friends, but theres a whole community to gain.

Once I started sharing my sobriety on social media and in my books, it was like people came out of the woodwork. I received emails, comments, messages, and support daily from people around the world. I realized that the sober community was f***ing amazing and full of some incredible human beings. They have supported me, encouraged me, rallied for me, and been a huge part of my journey.

Connect with the community.

Whether its at meetings, in person, in online support groups, or on social media, take advantage of this amazing group of people. It will blow your mind just how many people there are out there just like you and I. Find them. Use them. Support them. Connect with them.

You've got a lot more sober friends than you realize.

21. a new respect for your BODY

Destroying your body with alcohol is not respecting it.

When you are drinking large amounts, you're not being respectful to your body. You're actually treating it like absolute s*** instead. From your liver to your skin to your brain, alcohol is damaging. The things we put our body through when we abuse alcohol can have both immediate and long term effects that are very undesirable.

Were you treating your body well?

I put my body through the ringer during my drinking days. Not only did I get physically hurt multiple times from falling or collapsing while intoxicated, but I also was harming my body on the inside to the point that I had inflammation in my blood stream and early arthritis because of it. Now that I'm sober, I respect my body and treat it with respect and care instead.

Respect your body. You only have one.

In sobriety, we often gain this newfound respect for our body. We realize all that the body can be and do for us. We realize just how much we were abusing it. We now want to show it respect, especially after we think back on how much we did the opposite of that in the past.

Take care of your body. Be good to it.

22. feeling EMPOWERED as F***

There is just something empowering about being sober.

Nothing about getting wasted is empowering. Abusing alcohol and not trying to do anything to change doesn't leave you feeling motivated, inspired, and strong. It leaves you constantly saying you know you need to change but never taking the steps to actually get help and make that change. That doesn't feel empowering. Getting sober on the other hand, now that is empowering as f***.

It takes a lot of strength and a lot of fight to choose sobriety.

Once I got more comfortable in my sobriety, I grew to have a lot of pride about it. Knowing that I chose to change my life for the better made me feel so good inside. It showed me that I was able to better myself and to better my life all along...I just had to choose it and actually do it. It's been one of the most (if not THE most) empowering things I've done so far in my life.

Feel proud of yourself for choosing to be sober.

Remember what it took to get here. Don't forget how hard you've worked to better yourself by getting sober. You worked your a** off day in and day out. That's something to be hella proud of. That's something to feel empowered as f*** about!

YOU did this. YOU chose this. YOU made it happen.

23. learning to COPE without alcohol

"Coping" with alcohol doesn't solve anything.

Turning to alcohol for a solution to your problems never actually solves them. Sure, it might drown them away or numb them out for a while, but they always come back to the surface. That just creates a vicious and dangerous cycle of continuously abusing substances in an attempt to fix things without ever actually fixing them.

There are so many better ways to deal with your s***.

Trust me, I was the queen of trying to cope with alcohol. I leaned on it often when I didn't want to feel or deal with something I didn't like. After getting sober, I was determined to find new, healthier ways to cope with and deal with things. Finding those new coping mechanisms was a game changer. It also helped me move past a lot of things that I struggled with from my past.

Sobriety requires you to find healthier ways to cope.

You get to figure out what works for you with this one. Learning what things will help you navigate the difficult feelings and situations in life is extremely valuable. It helps you take control of things that are difficult and not be completely derailed by them.

Deal with your s***, but in a way that actually works.

24. not having to APOLOGIZE

Having to apologize for the things you did or said sucks.

I'm sure you all know the feeling all too well. It feels terrible having to constantly apologize for the things you said or did while you were drunk. Alcohol just makes you into someone that you usually aren't. That means you say and do things that you wouldn't normally do. This causes you to feel guilt, regret, and shame.

Now you never have to apologize on alcohol's behalf.

Having to apologize to people for the person I was when I was drunk was embarrassing. I woke up with so much regret on a regular basis. "I wish I didn't do that..." or "WHY did I say that!?" were often things I asked myself the next day. I do NOT miss that feeling one bit. I love knowing now that everything I say or do is because I intentionally chose to.

You get to control everything you do.

You have control over everything you choose to say or do now. That means you get to choose how you act and how you treat those around you. You can choose exactly what you want to say. You can choose to be a better person. You can choose the right things now.

Next time you apologize for something, it won't be because of alcohol.

25. getting to celebrate MILESTONES

Who doesn't love to celebrate!?

Many of your past celebrations probably involved alcohol, but not this one! Seriously, everyone loves celebrating. Whether it's your birthday, your anniversary, your new job, or in this case...YOUR SOBER ANNIVERSARY! There are so many celebrations and milestones in your sober journey, and every single one feels f***ing awesome. Celebrate all of them!

30 Days. 90 Days. 365 Days. 5,879 Days.

Celebrating my milestones in sobriety was something I began to look forward to every single time. I always feel so proud and so accomplished with each one I get to celebrate. Hey, it's just another celebration to mark on your calendar...and, personally, I can never have too many of those!

Celebrate every single milestone in your journey.

You deserve parades, balloons, confetti cannons, and cupcakes for every single milestone in your sobriety. Because it's not always easy. Sometimes it's really f***ing hard. Celebrate every single chance that you can, because you f***ing deserve it. YOU did all of this. You've worked your a** off for all of this.

Let the celebrations begin.

26. the opportunity to HELP OTHERS

We can't do it all on our own.

A lot of us like to think we can be successful in sobriety without any help. This might be true for like .5% of the sober community, but for most of us, we need the help. Whether its AA meetings, a sponsor, your therapist, or a friend or loved one that supported you through it all...we can use all the help we can get during this journey.

You've got the chance to pay it forward now.

Having the opportunity to use my story to help others out there in sobriety has been hands down THE most rewarding thing. Knowing that I can help others with what I've been through is a gift. It would almost feel selfish to NOT do this. People helped me get to where I am, and now it's my turn to return the favor and do the same for others.

You have the opportunity to help someone else change their life.

Connect with others in the sobriety community that might need some extra support. Use what you have been through. Share your knowledge, growth, and experiences with those that may need to hear it. You have a chance to share your journey and help someone else in theirs. You could even help save someone's life.

Turn your mess into your message.

27. lots of spiritual GROWTH

Let's get spiritual.

When you get your head really clear, your brain just works differently. Without alcohol bogging it down, you can think at a totally new, elevated level. This can open the doors of your spirituality wide open. It can be a little "woo woo" and "out there" to some, but connecting with yourself on a spiritual level can be extremely powerful for your personal growth.

Welcome the "woo woo" stuff.

I got ALL into my spirituality when I got sober. Honestly, it felt like something was just awakened inside of me. I was so curious about all of these new things I discovered and learned about myself. I got into tarot cards, energy healing, palm readers, signs from the Universe, prayer, and so many other things. It's actually quite interesting to learn about and explore.

Get ready for some serious spiritual growth.

Sobriety allows us think at a higher level. Its allows us to get in tune with our spiritual self and achieve crazy spiritual growth. You've probably never felt so in tune, aligned, and connected with yourself deep inside than ever before, right? It's a hella powerful thing! Embrace it!

Get in tune with your spiritual side and watch the magic that unfolds.

28. NOT having to HIDE anything

We're not hiding anything anymore.

When we struggle with addiction, we often try to hide it. Why? We feel ashamed, embarrassed, and we don't want others to see just how bad it really is. It's a constant act of trying to make it appear like we haven't totally lost control. We try to make others think its not as bad as it really is. Pretending to be something we aren't is exhausting.

You get to be your true self now.

There was something that felt so freeing to me when I finally owned ALL of my sobriety. I put my whole story out there. I shared all of my struggles. I celebrated my sober journey. It was liberating and freeing to no longer feel like I had to hide any part of myself, my past, or my journey. I got to just live and be me. It felt f***ing amazing.

How freeing it is to never have to hide again.

You are free to be you and to share that with the world. You never have to hide yourself or your alcohol use again. How incredible does that feel!? Knowing that you can live every single day of your life in your truth, authentically, and unapologetically.

Share the most authentic version of you.

29. feeling BRAVE as F***

Sobriety takes bravery.

Getting sober is definitely not for the weak, the scared, or the unsure. It takes a level of bravery, strength, and determination that you never knew you possessed. It would be the easy way out to just keep doing what you were doing, but you chose to be brave. You chose to face alcohol head on and go to war for yourself.

The battle is hard, but SO possible to win.

I didn't realize my bravery right away. It wasn't until I started sharing my story that people made it more clear to me. Sharing my journey took a huge leap of faith and whole lot of guts. I realized over time that it required not only bravery, but it also took heart, strength, and the desire for MORE for myself.

Suit up for battle in your shining armor.

You are SO brave for choosing this path, and you need to know that. You need to remind yourself of that at times. You chose the harder path. You chose the more difficult road. You chose to be brave and go to battle for yourself. You are your own f***ing hero. If you didn't realize that already, it's time you did.

You are strong. You are fearless. You are brave as f*.**

30. REAL
happiness

It's time to feel REAL happiness.

At one point, you may have thought alcohol made you happy. Most of us realize later that it wasn't making us happy at all...at least not real happiness. We may have been happy when we started drinking, but definitely did not feel that way afterwards. It's time to feel happiness that is REAL and lasting.

The sun will shine out of your a** again.

There have been many moments in my sober life where I truly stop and think, "Is it possible to be THIS happy?" I've realized that the answer to that question is a big fat HELL YES. I've created a life that makes me feel REAL happiness every single day when I wake up. I have been able to turn my life into one that I truly love and enjoy.

Real happiness is possible every single day.

Every day in sobriety has the opportunity to be the best day of your life. To live a life that is overflowing with happiness, joy, and all the good vibes possible. To feel healthy and happy each and every day. You've come so far and worked so hard...now it's time to enjoy it. That's something to be hella happy about.

Live healthy, happy, and full of gratitude.

31. so much GRATITUDE

There is SO much to be grateful for.

Overcoming your issues and addictions offers you so many incredible things in life. It allows you to escape the cycle. It allows you to grow as a person. It allows you to live your life free from the grip of alcohol and addiction. You have the choice to life your life any way you choose now, and that is something to be forever grateful for.

Give gratitude daily.

This is something I practice in my sobriety on a daily basis. Every morning I take a few minutes to say "THANK YOU" to God, the Universe, whatever Higher Powers there are out there, and also to myself for my sobriety. I will forever be grateful for where I have been able to get and for the life I get to live now. I make sure I recognize it daily.

What are you truly grateful for?

Give gratitude and give it often. When you are living sober, there is so much to feel grateful for. At times it can be almost overwhelming. Make sure to take a few minutes daily to show gratitude for what you have been able to achieve. Give gratitude for how much you have been able to change.

Give gratitude for this second chance at life.

32. FREEDOM

FREEDOM AT LAST.

Alcohol is a very controlling substance. If you allow it to, it will take every bit of freedom away from you. It will take over your life. It will destroy your dreams. It will never let you go...unless you take back control. When you choose sobriety, you choose to take your life back. You choose to live your life. You choose yourself, over and over again. You choose true FREEDOM.

You'll never feel more free as you do when you get sober.

Living in sobriety has given me back all of my freedom and more. I am free to live my life to the fullest. I am free to choose what my days look like. I am free to decide what I will do, who I will become, and how I will exist in this world. Sobriety has been the most freeing thing I've ever felt.

What will you do with the freedom?

You are f***ing FREE. You are free from the grip of alcohol. You are free from the cycle of addiction. You are free from the self-destructive patterns, the rock bottoms, and the helpless, hopeless feelings you once felt. There is no limit for what you can be, do, and achieve now. The freedom of sobriety is f***ing beautiful.

YOU ARE FINALLY FREE.

About The Author

As an entrepreneur, makeup artist, self-published author, YouTuber, mindset coach, podcast host, and blogger, Sarah Ordo is your not-so-average Millennial craving to leave her mark on this world in more ways than one.

Sarah's award-winning on location hair and makeup company (based out of Detroit), *24Luxe Hair & Makeup*, has been styling women for their special events since 2013. Her social media pages reach thousands of followers daily featuring a variety of beauty, health, lifestyle, sobriety, and wellness posts. Her YouTube videos documenting and following her sobriety have reached millions of viewers internationally, and have even been featured on Dateline NBC. Sarah has been featured on and interviewed for numerous blogs and podcasts including Cara Alwill Leyba's *Style Your Mind* Podcast and Courtney Bentley's *Fit Fierce & Fabulous* Podcast.

On her podcast *Her Best F***ing Life*, Sarah loves to talk about all topics surrounding how to create a life you love, your best life possible. The episodes feature a no-bullsh*t approach to life, amazing guest interviews, and a whole lot of swearing. On her website, *sarahordo.com*, Sarah blogs about living sober, self-love, mental health, and many other raw, honest topics. She also sells merchandise on her website for her books and podcast.

*Sober as F*** was the first full-length memoir and book written by Sarah, released in May 2017. She has gone on to publish *Innerbloom, Sober As F***:The Workbook,* the *Her Best F***ing Life Planner*, and *Thirty as F***,* which are all available on Amazon & Kindle.

Connect with Sarah: www.sarahordo.com
Youtube: Sarah Ordo
Instagram: @24Luxe_Sarah
Podcast: Her Best F***ing Life (on iTunes & Stitcher)
Books: Amazon & Kindle

66198146R00075

Made in the USA
Middletown, DE
05 September 2019